D0006691

# A Look at Kenya

## by Helen Frost

Consulting Editor: Gail Saunders-Smith, Ph.D.

Consultant: Lynette Jackson, Ph.D.
Assistant Professor of African History
Barnard College/Columbia University
New York City

## Pebble Books

an imprint of Capstone Press
Mankato, Minnesota

Pebble Books are published by Capstone Press
151 Good Counsel Drive, P.O. Box 669, Mankato, Minnesota 56002
http://www.capstone-press.com

2 3 4 5 6 07 06 05 04 03 02

*Library of Congress Cataloging-in-Publication Data*
Frost, Helen, 1949–
    A look at Kenya / by Helen Frost.
    p. cm.—(Our world)
    Includes bibliographical references and index.
    ISBN 0-7368-0984-8 (hardcover)
    ISBN 0-7368-4853-3 (paperback)
    1. Kenya—Juvenile literature. [1. Kenya.] I. Title. II. Series: Our world (Pebble
Books)
DT433.522.F76 2002
967.62—dc21                                                                    00-012779

Summary: Simple text and photographs depict the land, animals, and people
of Kenya.

## Note to Parents and Teachers

The Our World series supports national social studies standards
related to culture. This book describes and illustrates the land,
animals, and people of Kenya. The photographs support early
readers in understanding the text. The repetition of words and
phrases helps early readers learn new words. This book also
introduces early readers to subject-specific vocabulary words, which
are defined in the Words to Know section. Early readers may need
assistance to read some words and to use the Table of Contents,
Words to Know, Read More, Internet Sites, and Index/Word List
sections of the book.

# Table of Contents

# Kenya

★ Nairobi

Kenya is on the east coast of Africa. The capital of Kenya is Nairobi. Nairobi is the largest city in Kenya.

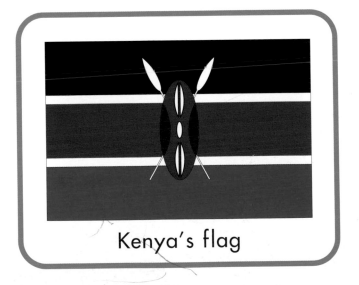

Kenya's flag

Kenya is warmest near the coast. Kenya is cooler in the mountains. Kenya has a rainy season and a dry season.

giraffe

hippos

8

Giraffes, elephants, lions, and zebras live on Kenya's savannas. Hippos and crocodiles live in Kenya's rivers.

More than 30 million
people live in Kenya.
Some Kenyans live
in cities. Most Kenyans
live in the country.

Kiswahili and English
are Kenya's official
languages. Students learn
both languages in school.

Some Kenyans like to run. Runners from Kenya have won races all around the world. Kenyans also like to play soccer.

Some Kenyans fish or guide tourists to earn money. Some Kenyan farmers grow coffee, tea, and sugarcane.

Kenya's money is counted in shillings.

Some Kenyans have cars. Most Kenyans walk, run, or take a bus.

20

Scientists have found very old human bones in Kenya. They think that the world's first people may have lived in Kenya.

# Words to Know

**Africa**—one of the seven continents of the world; Africa is located between the Atlantic Ocean and the Indian Ocean.

**capital**—the city in a country where the government is based; the capital of Kenya is Nairobi.

**Kiswahili**—one of Kenya's official languages; many other languages are also spoken in Kenya.

**savanna**—a flat, grassy plain; many wild animals and birds live on Kenya's savannas.

**shilling**—the money used in Kenya; shillings are also used in other countries; the shilling in Kenya is called the Kenyan shilling (KSh).

**tourist**—someone who travels and visits places for fun, relaxation, or adventure

## Read More

**Dahl, Michael.** *Kenya.* Countries of the World. Mankato, Minn.: Bridgestone Books, 1997.

**Gresko, Marcia S.** *Kenya.* Letters Home From. Woodbridge, Conn.: Blackbirch Press, 1999.

**McCollum, Sean.** *Kenya.* Globetrotters Club. Minneapolis: Carolrhoda Books, 1999.

**Ryan, Patrick.** *Kenya.* Faces and Places. Chanhassen, Minn.: Child's World, 1999.

## Internet Sites

**Africa Online: Kenya**
http://www.africaonline.co.ke/AfricaOnline/coverkids.html

**Introduction to Kenya**
http://www.geographia.com/kenya

**World Safari**
http://www.supersurf.com

# Index/Word List

Africa, 5
bones, 21
city, 5, 11
coast, 5, 7
country, 11
crocodiles, 9
elephants, 9
English, 13
farmers, 17

giraffes, 9
hippos, 9
Kenyans, 11, 15, 17, 19
Kiswahili, 13
languages, 13
lions, 9
money, 17
mountains, 7

Nairobi, 5
people, 11, 21
rivers, 9
savannas, 9
scientists, 21
tourists, 17
world, 15
zebras, 9

**Word Count: 161**
**Early-Intervention Level: 18**

**Editorial Credits**
Mari C. Schuh, editor; Kia Bielke, cover designer and illustrator; Kimberly Danger, photo researcher

**Photo Credits**
Bettmann/CORBIS, 20
Corel, 8 (left)
Michele Burgess, cover, 12
Photo Network/Howard Folsom, 10
Photri-Microstock, 16
Pictor/Paul Conklin, 18
Stan Osolinski/Root Resources, 1
Trip/W. Jacobs, 6 (top)
Unicorn Stock Photos/Rod Furgason, 6 (bottom)
Visuals Unlimited/Barbara Gerlach, 8 (right)
Yann Arthus-Bertrand/CORBIS, 14

The author thanks the children's section staff at the Allen County Public Library in Fort Wayne, Indiana, for research assistance.